KATHLEEN BAILEY

The Budtender's Handbook

Essential Skills for Success in the Cannabis Retail Space

First edition

ISBN: 978-1-961408-13-5

This book was professionally typeset on Reedsy.
Find out more at reedsy.com

Contents

1

Introduction

The cannabis industry has experienced significant growth and change in recent years, driven by a wave of legalization and increasing public acceptance around the world. As the industry continues to evolve and expand, there is a rising demand for knowledgeable, skilled, and professional individuals to fill roles in dispensaries and retail outlets. One of the most vital roles in this blossoming field is that of the budtender.

Budtenders are at the forefront of the cannabis retail experience, serving as ambassadors to customers and providing valuable guidance on products and consumption methods. Their unique position at the intersection of customer service and product expertise makes them an essential component of a successful dispensary. The importance of a quality budtender cannot be overstated, as their interactions with customers have a significant impact on the overall customer experience and, ultimately, the success of the business.

In this book, we will explore the various aspects of becoming a quality budtender, covering a wide range of topics from the fundamentals of cannabis to advanced customer service techniques. You will learn about the history of cannabis and its role in society, as well as the various cannabinoids, terpenes, and consumption methods that make up the diverse world of cannabis products. We will also delve into the specific duties and responsibilities of a budtender, as well as the essential tools and equipment necessary to excel in the role.

Furthermore, we will discuss effective communication strategies to engage with customers and provide tailored recommendations, ensuring a positive and memorable experience for each individual. Staying up-to-date on industry trends, products, and regulations is crucial, and we will offer guidance on how to remain informed and adaptable in this rapidly changing landscape.

Lastly, we will address the importance of ethics and social responsibility in the cannabis industry, emphasizing the need for promoting responsible consumption, advocating for social equity, and supporting environmental sustainability.

Whether you are an aspiring budtender looking to enter the industry or an experienced professional seeking to refine your skills, this book aims to provide you with the comprehensive knowledge and practical guidance necessary to thrive in the world of cannabis retail. Join us as we embark on this journey to becoming a quality budtender and explore the exciting opportunities that await in the rapidly growing cannabis industry.

2

History of Cannabis and Dispensaries

Brief history of cannabis use and legalization

Cannabis has a long and rich history, with evidence of its use dating back thousands of years. Ancient cultures in Asia, Africa, and the Americas utilized the plant for medicinal, spiritual, and recreational purposes. Some of the earliest recorded uses of cannabis date back to ancient China, where it was utilized for its therapeutic properties and as a source of fiber for clothing and paper. Over time, cannabis spread across the globe, and its use continued to grow in popularity.

However, the 20th century saw a shift in attitudes toward cannabis, as many countries, including the United States, began to criminalize its possession and use. This change was driven by a combination of political, social, and economic factors, as well as misconceptions about the plant's effects on health and behavior. The stigmatization of cannabis led to widespread prohibition, with a focus on law enforcement and punitive measures.

The tide began to turn in the late 20th and early 21st centuries as advocates pushed for the reevaluation of cannabis laws. In the United States, the movement gained momentum in the 1990s, when states such as California began legalizing cannabis for medical use. Scientific research demonstrated the potential therapeutic benefits of cannabis, leading to a renewed interest in its medical applications. This evidence, along with growing public support, paved the way for the gradual legalization of cannabis for medical and, in some cases, recreational use in various countries and U.S. states.

Evolution of dispensaries

As the legal landscape shifted, the need for a regulated system to distribute cannabis became apparent. The first modern medical cannabis dispensaries emerged in the 1990s in response to the growing demand for safe and legal access to the plant for patients with qualifying medical conditions.

These early dispensaries often operated in a legal gray area, as they faced opposition from law enforcement and fluctuating regulations. However, as more states and countries embraced medical cannabis, the industry evolved, and dispensaries began to professionalize their operations.

With the advent of recreational legalization in some regions, dispensaries have continued to evolve, becoming more sophisticated and customer-focused. Today's dispensaries offer a wide range of products, from flower to edibles and topicals, catering to the diverse needs of both medical and recreational consumers. Modern dispensaries also prioritize customer education and emphasize the importance of responsible consumption, reflecting a growing commitment to the well-being of their clientele.

Legal status and regulations

The legal status of cannabis varies significantly from country to country and, in the United States, from state to state. While some regions have fully legalized cannabis for recreational use, others only permit its use for medical purposes or maintain strict prohibition.

In areas where cannabis is legal, a complex framework of regulations governs its cultivation, distribution, and sale. These regulations often include strict licensing requirements for businesses, extensive product testing and labeling standards, and rules governing advertising and marketing practices. Compliance with these regulations is essential for dispensaries and budtenders to operate legally and maintain a positive reputation in the industry.

It is crucial for budtenders to remain informed about the specific regulations in their jurisdiction, as these rules can change over time. Additionally, budtenders must be aware of the varying legal status of cannabis in different locations, as this knowledge can inform their interactions with customers, particularly those visiting from other regions.

In summary, understanding the history of cannabis and dispensaries, as well as the legal status and regulations governing the industry, is a vital foundation for any aspiring budtender. This knowledge provides context for the budtender's role and highlights the importance of professionalism and compliance in the evolving world of cannabis retail.

3

The Basics of Cannabis

Understanding cannabinoids (THC, CBD, etc.)

Cannabinoids are the naturally occurring chemical compounds found in the cannabis plant that interact with the human body's endocannabinoid system. This system plays a crucial role in regulating various physiological processes, including mood, appetite, pain sensation, and immune response. Over 100 cannabinoids have been identified, but the two most well-known and widely researched are THC (tetrahydrocannabinol) and CBD (cannabidiol).

THC is the primary psychoactive compound in cannabis, responsible for producing the characteristic "high" associated with its consumption. It can induce feelings of euphoria, relaxation, and increased sensory perception, but may also cause side effects such as anxiety and paranoia in some individuals.

CBD, on the other hand, is non-psychoactive and has gained popularity for its potential therapeutic benefits, which include pain relief, anti inflammatory effects, and anxiety reduction. CBD is often used to counterbalance the psychoactive effects of THC, leading to a more balanced and controlled experience.

Other cannabinoids, such as CBG (cannabigerol), CBN (cannabinol), and THCV (tetrahydrocannabivarin), have also shown promise for various therapeutic applications, but more research is needed to fully understand their effects and potential uses.

Cannabis strains: Indica, Sativa, and Hybrids

Cannabis plants are traditionally classified into two primary types: Indica and Sativa. Indica strains are known for their relaxing and sedative effects, often recommended for evening use or to alleviate stress and anxiety. They typically have a higher CBD to THC ratio, contributing to their calming properties.

Sativa strains, conversely, are associated with uplifting and energizing effects, making them suitable for daytime use or to stimulate creativity and focus. Sativas generally have a higher THC to CBD ratio, which can produce more pronounced psychoactive effects.

Hybrid strains are a combination of Indica and Sativa genetics, offering a blend of effects that can vary depending on the specific parent strains. Hybrids are often bred to achieve specific desired characteristics, such as particular flavors, aromas, or effects, and can be tailored to meet individual preferences.

It is important to note that the Indica-Sativa distinction is an oversim-plification, as the effects of a given strain are influenced by a variety of factors, including individual genetics, terpene profiles, and cultivation techniques.

Terpenes and their effects

Terpenes are naturally occurring aromatic compounds found in cannabis and many other plants. They are responsible for the distinct smells and flavors that help differentiate various cannabis strains. In addition to contributing to the sensory experience of cannabis, terpenes also play a significant role in the plant's overall effects and potential therapeutic benefits. They interact with cannabinoids to produce what is known as the "entourage effect," a synergistic relationship that can enhance or modify the overall effects of the cannabis product. Some common terpenes found in cannabis and their associated properties include:

- **Myrcene:** Known for its earthy, musky aroma, myrcene is one of the most abundant terpenes found in cannabis. It is believed to have sedative and muscle-relaxing effects, potentially contributing to the calming and relaxing properties of some strains. Myrcene may also have anti-inflammatory and analgesic properties, making it potentially beneficial for pain relief.
- **Limonene:** Characterized by a bright, citrusy aroma, limonene is a prevalent terpene in many Sativa-dominant strains. It is thought to have uplifting and mood-enhancing effects, potentially contributing to the energetic and invigorating properties of certain cannabis varieties. Additionally, limonene has been studied for its potential anti-anxiety, anti-depressant, and immune-boosting properties.
- **Pinene:** As the name suggests, pinene is known for its pine-like aroma and is one of the most common terpenes found in nature. It is thought to have potential anti-inflammatory, bronchodilatory

and memory-enhancing effects. Pinene may counteract some of the short-term memory impairment associated with THC, potentially contributing to a more focused and clear-headed cannabis experience.

- **Linalool:** Recognizable by its floral and slightly sweet aroma, linalool is a terpene commonly found in lavender and other aromatic plants. Linalool is believed to have potential calming, sedative, and anti-anxiety effects, making it potentially beneficial for stress relief and relaxation. It may also have anti-inflammatory and analgesic properties, contributing to pain relief.
- **Caryophyllene:** Known for its spicy, peppery aroma, caryophyllene is unique among terpenes due to its ability to bind directly to cannabinoid receptors in the body. This interaction makes caryophyllene potentially useful for managing pain, inflammation, and anxiety. It has also been studied for its potential gastroprotective and anti-addiction properties.

Understanding the role and effects of terpenes is essential for budtenders, as this knowledge can inform tailored strain recommendations based on a customer's specific needs and preferences. By considering the terpene profiles of different strains, budtenders can better guide customers toward a cannabis product that may offer the desired aroma, flavor, and effects.

Various forms of consumption (smoking, vaping, edibles, tinctures, etc.)

Cannabis can be consumed in several ways, each with its own advantages and drawbacks. Understanding these methods is essential for budtenders to provide appropriate recommendations based on individual preferences and needs. Some popular methods include:

- **Smoking:** The traditional method of inhaling combusted cannabis flower, providing immediate effects but also exposing users to potentially harmful smoke and tar. This method is popular for its rapid onset and ease of use, but may not be suitable for those with respiratory issues or seeking a discreet consumption option.
- **Vaporizing (vaping):** Heating cannabis to release its active compounds without combustion, resulting in a cleaner and less harsh inhalation experience. Vaping can be done using dry herb vaporizers or vape pens with concentrated cannabis oil. This method is often preferred by those seeking a more discreet and potentially healthier alternative to smoking.
- **Edibles:** Cannabis-infused food products that are ingested, such as brownies, gummies, or beverages. The effects of edibles are generally slower to onset (30 minutes to 2 hours) and longer-lasting compared to inhalation methods, making them popular for those seeking sustained relief or a more controlled experience. However, dosage and potency can be more challenging to manage, particularly for inexperienced users.
- **Tinctures:** Liquid cannabis extracts, typically alcohol-based, that are taken sublingually (under the tongue) or added to food and beverages. Tinctures offer a precise dosing option and rapid onset, making them popular for medical users or those seeking a discreet and smoke-free consumption method.

- **Topicals:** Cannabis-infused creams, balms, and salves that are applied directly to the skin. Topicals are primarily used for localized pain relief, inflammation, and skin conditions, and do not typically produce psychoactive effects. This makes them an ideal option for those seeking targeted relief without the "high" associated with other consumption methods.

- **Concentrates:** Highly potent cannabis extracts, such as shatter, wax, or rosin, that can be vaporized, smoked, or added to edibles. Concentrates provide a more intense and rapid onset of effects, making them popular among experienced users seeking a stronger experience. However, due to their potency, concentrates may not be suitable for novice users or those with a low tolerance.

- **Capsules and pills:** Cannabis extracts in pill or capsule form, offering a precise and discreet dosing option. These products typically have a slower onset and more controlled release, making them popular for medical users seeking consistent and long-lasting relief.

As a budtender, it is crucial to understand the various forms of cannabis consumption and their unique characteristics in order to guide customers toward the most suitable method based on their preferences, experience, and desired effects. Providing accurate and tailored recommendations will help ensure a positive and satisfying experience for each individual.

4

Budtender Responsibilities and Duties

Sales Skills

Budtenders play a significant role in driving sales within a dispensary, making sales skills an essential aspect of their responsibilities and duties. By combining their in-depth product knowledge with effective sales techniques, budtenders can successfully guide customers towards the most suitable products while contributing to the overall profitability of the dispensary.

Building rapport with customers: Developing strong relationships with customers is the foundation of successful sales. Budtenders should engage customers in a friendly and approachable manner, making them feel welcome and valued. By asking open-ended questions and showing genuine interest in their needs and preferences, budtenders can create a trusting connection that fosters repeat business and customer loyalty

Identifying customer needs and preferences: To effectively recommend products, budtenders must first understand the customer's specific requirements, preferences, and experience levels. By actively listening and asking targeted questions, budtenders can gain valuable insights into the customer's desired effects, preferred consumption methods, and budget constraints. This information enables them to make personalized and relevant recommendations that align with the customer's unique needs.

Upselling and cross-selling: Budtenders should be skilled in the art of upselling and cross-selling, which involves suggesting additional or alternative products that complement the customer's initial selection. By presenting customers with a range of options, budtenders can not only enhance the customer's overall experience but also increase the average transaction value. To achieve this, budtenders must be knowledgeable about the full range of products available in the dispensary, as well as any promotions or discounts that may be applicable.

Overcoming objections: Occasionally, customers may express concerns or objections regarding a product's price, potency, or suitability. Budtenders must be prepared to address these concerns by providing clear and informative explanations, highlighting the product's unique benefits, and offering alternative solutions if necessary. By effectively overcoming objections, budtenders can instill confidence in the customer's decision and ultimately close the sale.

Closing the sale: Once a customer has received personalized recommendations and expressed interest in a product, budtenders should guide them through the final steps of the transaction. This includes confirming the order, processing payment, and providing any necessary information about the product's usage, storage, and safety guidelines. By ensuring a smooth and efficient checkout process, budtenders can leave a lasting positive impression on the customer, encouraging them to return for future purchases.

Sales skills are a crucial component of a budtender's responsibilities and duties. By combining their product knowledge with effective sales techniques, budtenders can successfully guide customers towards suitable products while contributing to the overall success and profitability of the dispensary.

Customer Service Skills

Customer service skills are a vital responsibility and duty for budtenders in the cannabis industry. As the primary point of contact between customers and the dispensary, budtenders play a crucial role in shaping the overall customer experience. Their ability to provide exceptional service directly impacts customer satisfaction, loyalty, and the reputation of the dispensary. Providing friendly, attentive, and informative service is essential for building lasting relationships with customers and ensuring they leave the dispensary with a positive impression.

One of the most important customer service skills for budtenders is active listening. By carefully listening to customers' questions, concerns, and preferences, budtenders can better understand their needs and provide tailored recommendations. Active listening also involves paying attention to non-verbal cues and asking follow-up questions, allowing budtenders to gain a deeper understanding of each customer's unique situation. This level of attention and care demonstrates genuine concern for the customer's well-being and helps build trust between the budtender and the customer.

Patience and empathy are also crucial customer service skills for budtenders. Many customers entering a dispensary may be inexperienced or apprehensive about using cannabis, and it is the budtender's responsibility to create a welcoming and non-judgmental environment. By showing patience and understanding, budtenders can help customers feel more at ease and comfortable discussing their needs. Empathy enables budtenders to put themselves in the customer's shoes, allowing them to provide more compassionate and informed guidance, which ultimately leads to a better customer experience.

Finally, effective communication is essential for providing excellent customer service as a budtender. This involves not only speaking clearly and confidently but also conveying complex information about cannabis products in a way that is easy for customers to understand. Budtenders must be adept at explaining the differences between strains, consumption methods, and dosages, ensuring that customers have all the information they need to make informed decisions. By honing their communication skills, budtenders can empower customers with knowledge and confidence, contributing to a positive and memorable dispensary experience.

Product Knowledge

Product knowledge is an essential responsibility for budtenders in the cannabis industry, as it enables them to provide accurate and valuable information to customers. With a wide variety of strains, consumption methods, and products available in the market, budtenders must be well-versed in the characteristics and effects of each offering in order to guide customers towards the best possible choices. A deep understanding of cannabis products not only ensures that customers receive the most suitable recommendations but also helps establish the budtender as a reliable and trustworthy source of information.

Budtenders should have a comprehensive understanding of the various strains of cannabis, including their unique properties and effects. This includes knowing the differences between Indica, Sativa, and hybrid strains, as well as their typical cannabinoid and terpene profiles. By being knowledgeable about the specific effects and medical benefits associated with each strain, budtenders can confidently recommend the most appropriate options to customers based on their needs, preferences, and experience levels.

Additionally, budtenders must possess extensive knowledge of the different consumption methods and forms of cannabis products available. This includes understanding the nuances of smoking, vaping, edibles, tinctures, topicals, and concentrates, as well as their respective advantages and drawbacks. Budtenders should also be familiar with proper dosing guidelines and onset times for each consumption method, ensuring that customers have the information they need to consume cannabis safely and effectively. This level of expertise allows budtenders to provide personalized recommendations that take into account the customer's specific situation and preferences.

Staying up-to-date with the latest cannabis products and trends is also a crucial aspect of a budtender's product knowledge responsibility. The cannabis industry is constantly evolving, with new products, brands, and technologies emerging regularly. Budtenders should be proactive in staying informed about these developments by attending industry events, participating in training sessions, and researching new products. This commitment to continuous learning allows budtenders to remain at the forefront of the industry, providing customers with the most current and relevant information to make informed decisions about their cannabis consumption.

Inventory Management

Effective inventory management is crucial for budtenders to ensure that products are adequately stocked, well-organized, and properly displayed. Budtenders must be familiar with their dispensary's inventory system and be able to efficiently locate and retrieve products for customers. Additionally, budtenders should be vigilant about monitoring product freshness and quality, promptly addressing any issues that may arise. Proper inventory management helps maintain a professional and appealing retail environment, ultimately contributing to a positive customer experience.

Compliance with Local and State Regulations

Adhering to local and state regulations is essential for budtenders to maintain a safe and legally compliant work environment. This includes verifying customer identification, ensuring proper product labeling, and following established protocols for handling and selling cannabis products. Budtenders must stay informed about current and changing regulations in their jurisdiction, as non-compliance can result in serious consequences for both the individual and the dispensary.

Safe Handling Practices

Budtenders are responsible for handling cannabis products safely and hygienically, minimizing the risk of contamination and ensuring product quality. This includes wearing gloves when handling flower, using proper tools and equipment, and maintaining a clean and organized workspace. Budtenders should also be knowledgeable about proper storage conditions for various cannabis products to preserve their freshness, potency, and overall quality.

Budtenders play a critical role in the cannabis retail experience, and their responsibilities extend far beyond simply selling products. By prioritizing customer service, product knowledge, inventory management, regulatory compliance, and safe handling practices, budtenders can create a welcoming and professional environment that fosters customer satisfaction and trust.

5

Effective Communication with Customers

Active listening and empathy

E ffective communication with customers begins with active listening and empathy. Budtenders must be attentive to customers' questions, concerns, and preferences, taking the time to fully understand their needs before offering recommendations. By demonstrating empathy and genuine interest in the customer's experience, budtenders can build trust and establish a strong rapport that leads to more satisfying interactions.

Tailoring recommendations to individual needs

Each customer's needs and preferences are unique, and budtenders must be adept at tailoring their recommendations accordingly. This involves considering factors such as the customer's experience with cannabis, desired effects, potential medical benefits, and preferred consumption method. By offering personalized guidance, budtenders can ensure that customers feel valued and supported in their cannabis journey, ultimately leading to greater satisfaction and loyalty.

Educating customers on responsible consumption

As knowledgeable professionals, budtenders have a responsibility to educate customers on responsible cannabis consumption. This includes providing information on proper dosing, the differences between strains and products, and potential side effects or interactions. By promoting responsible consumption, budtenders can help customers make informed decisions and minimize the risk of negative experiences.

Handling difficult situations

Budtenders may occasionally encounter challenging situations, such as customers who are visibly intoxicated, unruly, or dissatisfied with their purchase. In these instances, it is essential for budtenders to remain calm, composed, and professional. Effective communication techniques, such as de-escalation and conflict resolution, can help defuse tensions and ensure a safe and pleasant environment for all customers. In some cases, budtenders may need to involve a manager or security personnel to address the situation appropriately.

Effective communication with customers is a crucial aspect of a budtender's role in the cannabis industry. By practicing active listening, empathy, and tailored recommendations, budtenders can create positive and meaningful connections with customers. Furthermore, by promoting responsible consumption and addressing difficult situations with professionalism, budtenders can help ensure a safe and enjoyable experience for all.

6

Essential Budtender Tools

Weighing and measuring equipment

Accurate weighing and measuring equipment are essential tools for budtenders, ensuring that customers receive the correct amount of product and helping maintain inventory control. Digital scales are commonly used for their precision and ease of use. Budtenders should be proficient in operating and calibrating these scales, and ensure that they are regularly cleaned and maintained to guarantee accurate measurements.

Point of sale systems

Point of sale (POS) systems are crucial for managing sales transactions, customer information, and inventory. Budtenders must be familiar with their dispensary's POS system and be able to navigate it efficiently and accurately. A comprehensive understanding of the POS system allows budtenders to process transactions quickly, provide customers with detailed information about their purchase, and maintain accurate records for inventory and compliance purposes.

Proper storage and organization

Proper storage and organization are critical for maintaining product freshness, quality, and compliance with regulations. Budtenders should be knowledgeable about the appropriate storage conditions for various cannabis products, including temperature, humidity, and light exposure. Additionally, effective organization helps ensure that products are easily accessible and well-presented, contributing to a professional retail environment and streamlined customer experience.

Personal protective equipment (PPE)

Budtenders must use personal protective equipment (PPE) when handling cannabis products to minimize the risk of contamination and ensure compliance with local regulations. Common PPE items include gloves, face masks, and lab coats or aprons. By consistently utilizing PPE, budtenders can protect both themselves and their customers, promoting a safe and hygienic retail environment.

Having the right tools at their disposal enables budtenders to perform their duties efficiently and professionally. Weighing and measuring equipment, point of sale systems, proper storage and organization, and personal protective equipment are all essential components of a budtender's toolkit. By mastering the use of these tools, budtenders can provide an exceptional customer experience and maintain a safe, compliant, and efficient work environment.

7

Staying Updated on Industry Trends and Products

Following industry news and developments

As the cannabis industry is constantly evolving, budtenders must stay informed about the latest news and developments. This includes keeping up with changes in legislation, new products, and innovations in cultivation and consumption methods. Following reputable industry news sources, blogs, and social media platforms can help budtenders stay up-to-date on relevant information and be prepared to answer customer questions knowledgeably.

Participating in training and educational programs

Ongoing education is vital for budtenders to maintain and expand their knowledge of cannabis products, best practices, and industry trends. Participating in training sessions, workshops, webinars, and certification programs can provide valuable insights and enhance professional growth. Many dispensaries offer in-house training, while other organizations and educational institutions provide specialized courses tailored to the needs of cannabis industry professionals.

Networking with other professionals

Connecting with fellow budtenders, dispensary owners, cultivators, and other industry professionals can offer valuable insights and opportunities for learning. Networking can take place through industry events, conferences, online forums, and social media platforms. By building relationships with others in the field, budtenders can share experiences, discuss challenges, and stay informed about emerging trends and best practices.

Understanding and adapting to emerging trends

As customer preferences and market trends change, budtenders must be able to recognize and adapt to these shifts. This may involve learning about new product types, consumption methods, or strain genetics that are gaining popularity. Understanding these trends allows budtenders to make informed recommendations and provide customers with the most current and relevant information. By staying flexible and adaptable, budtenders can ensure that they continue to meet the evolving needs and expectations of their clientele.

Staying updated on industry trends and products is essential for budtenders to maintain their expertise and provide exceptional customer service. By following industry news, participating in ongoing education, networking with other professionals, and adapting to emerging trends, budtenders can ensure that they remain at the forefront of the rapidly evolving cannabis industry.

8

Building a Successful Budtender Career

Crafting a standout resume and cover letter

To make a strong impression on potential employers, budtenders must craft a standout resume and cover letter that highlight their relevant skills, experience, and qualifications. When creating a resume, emphasize customer service and sales experience, knowledge of cannabis products, and any training or certifications related to the industry. In the cover letter, focus on conveying enthusiasm for the role and explaining how your unique background and expertise make you an ideal candidate for the position.

Acing the interview process

The interview is a crucial opportunity for budtenders to showcase their knowledge, communication skills, and passion for the cannabis industry. To prepare, research the dispensary's products and operations, and familiarize yourself with common interview questions related to the role. During the interview, demonstrate your customer service skills by being friendly, engaging, and attentive. Be prepared to discuss your experience, knowledge of cannabis, and how you can contribute to the success of the dispensary.

Continuing education and professional development

As previously mentioned, ongoing education and professional development are essential for budtenders seeking career growth. By staying informed about industry trends, participating in training programs, and networking with other professionals, budtenders can continually expand their knowledge and enhance their expertise. This commitment to learning will not only improve job performance but also make budtenders more attractive candidates for promotions and advancement opportunities.

Opportunities for advancement within the industry

A successful budtender career can open the door to numerous advancement opportunities within the cannabis industry. With experience and a strong track record of performance, budtenders may progress into roles such as lead budtender, store manager, or even dispensary owner. Additionally, budtenders may choose to specialize in areas such as cultivation, extraction, product development, or sales, leveraging their industry knowledge and experience to excel in these fields.

Building a successful budtender career involves crafting a standout resume and cover letter, acing the interview process, and engaging in ongoing education and professional development. By demonstrating dedication, expertise, and a commitment to growth, budtenders can seize opportunities for advancement and enjoy a rewarding and fulfilling career in the cannabis industry.

9

Ethics and Social Responsibility

Promoting responsible consumption

Budtenders play an essential role in promoting responsible cannabis consumption. This includes educating customers about proper dosing, potential side effects, and safe storage practices. By providing accurate information and personalized guidance, budtenders can help minimize the risk of overconsumption, impaired driving, and other negative consequences. In doing so, they contribute to a safer, more responsible cannabis culture.

Advocating for social equity in the cannabis industry

The cannabis industry has a complex history involving racial and social disparities, particularly regarding the criminalization and enforcement of cannabis laws. Budtenders can advocate for social equity by supporting initiatives that promote diversity, inclusion, and equal opportunities within the industry. This may involve participating in advocacy efforts, supporting minority-owned businesses, or engaging in community outreach programs that address the historical injustices associated with cannabis prohibition.

Environmental sustainability

Environmental sustainability is an important consideration for the cannabis industry, given the potential impacts of cultivation, production, and waste disposal. Budtenders can contribute to sustainability efforts by promoting eco-friendly products, such as those that use organic cultivation methods or biodegradable packaging. Additionally, they can educate customers about proper disposal methods for cannabis waste and encourage the use of reusable accessories, such as refillable vape pens or storage containers.

Supporting local communities

Budtenders can help foster strong local communities by supporting local businesses and participating in community events. By sourcing products from local growers and manufacturers, dispensaries can contribute to the local economy and create a sense of community pride. Furthermore, dispensaries and budtenders can engage in charitable initiatives, such as sponsoring local events or partnering with nonprofits, to give back to their communities and demonstrate their commitment to social responsibility.

Ethics and social responsibility are crucial aspects of a budtender's role in the cannabis industry. By promoting responsible consumption, advocating for social equity, prioritizing environmental sustainability, and supporting local communities, budtenders can contribute to a more ethical and socially conscious cannabis culture. These efforts not only benefit the industry as a whole but also help to establish trust and credibility with customers, creating a positive and lasting impact.

10 .

Conclusion

Throughout this book, we have explored the various aspects of becoming a successful and knowledgeable budtender in the rapidly evolving cannabis industry. From understanding the history of cannabis and dispensaries to mastering the basics of cannabis products and their effects, budtenders must develop a strong foundation of knowledge to provide exceptional customer service and support.

Equally important are the responsibilities and duties associated with the role, including inventory management, compliance with local and state regulations, and safe handling practices. Effective communication with customers, active listening, and empathy are essential for building rapport and meeting the unique needs of each individual. Mastery of essential budtender tools, such as weighing and measuring equipment, POS systems, and proper storage practices, ensures a professional and efficient work environment.

Continual learning and professional development are key to staying updated on industry trends, products, and emerging opportunities. By networking with other professionals and participating in ongoing education, budtenders can advance their careers and seize new opportunities within the industry.

Lastly, a commitment to ethics and social responsibility is crucial for creating a positive and lasting impact in the cannabis industry. By promoting responsible consumption, advocating for social equity, prioritizing environmental sustainability, and supporting local communities, budtenders can contribute to a more ethical and socially conscious cannabis culture.

By following the guidance provided in this book, aspiring and experienced budtenders alike can develop the skills, knowledge, and professionalism required to excel in their roles and contribute to the continued growth and success of the cannabis industry. Embrace the opportunity to make a meaningful difference in the lives of your customers and your community, and embark on a rewarding and fulfilling career as a quality budtender.

Made in the USA
Monee, IL
08 December 2023

48647126R00022